Enemy Alien

Walter's Journey
Through Adversity

Written by Csilla Toldy,
based on the true-life story of Walter Sekules

Colour illustrations by Agnes Tamcsu

Published by Light Theatre Company CIC with support of
The National Lottery Heritage Fund, thanks to National
Lottery players and the Arts Council of Northern Ireland

ISBN: 978-1-3999-7811-8

Designed by April Sky Design, Newtownards
Printed by GPS Colour Graphics Ltd, Belfast

Contents

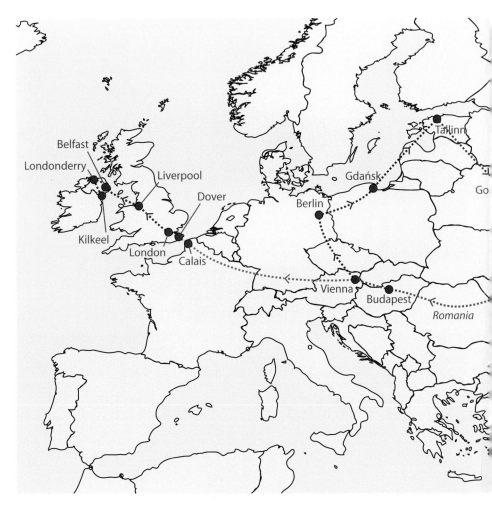

Map showing Walter Sekules' journey

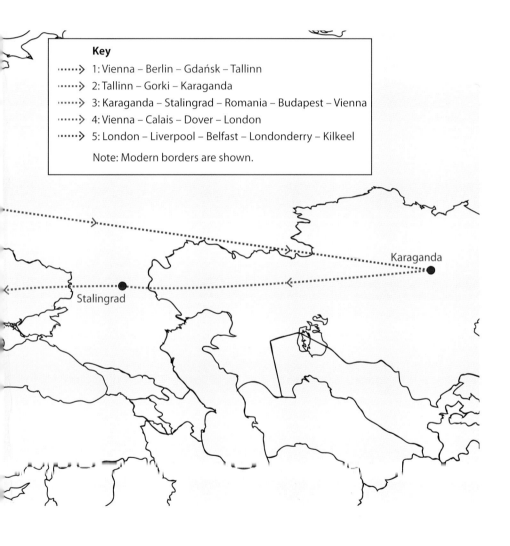

Key

·····⟩ 1: Vienna – Berlin – Gdańsk – Tallinn

·····⟩ 2: Tallinn – Gorki – Karaganda

·····⟩ 3: Karaganda – Stalingrad – Romania – Budapest – Vienna

·····⟩ 4: Vienna – Calais – Dover – London

·····⟩ 5: London – Liverpool – Belfast – Londonderry – Kilkeel

Note: Modern borders are shown.

Karaganda

Stalingrad

"Often in life, the darkest night turns into the brightest dawn."

Edith Sekules

Dedicated to the memory of Walter Sekules 1940–2023

This is the story of Walter Sekules, a Jewish boy who survived WWII in a prisoner-of-war camp in Siberia. He was born in Tallinn, Estonia on April 20, 1940. Strangely enough, he shared a birthday with Adolf Hitler, the man whose cruel policies drove his family away from their home in Vienna.

People say that the first eight years of your life are the most important in forming character.

Walter was grateful beyond measure for those years. He was grateful for the immense luck that helped him to survive the Holocaust, and his loving parents who made sure that his childhood was as innocent as any should be, even though in those first years of his life he was an Enemy Alien.

The times before Walter's birth

Walter's parents lived in Vienna, the capital of Austria, situated in the middle of Europe, at the feet of the Alps. Vienna was the centre of classical music and opera. Walter's mother, Edith, studied music. The family was not well-off and straight after finishing grammar school, she had to find a position at the Bristol Hotel in the city centre, where she worked a 60-hour week.

Walter's father, Kurt, was a radio engineer, a useful profession in the early days of this technology. Edith and Kurt were Jewish. In November 1935, they got married in a synagogue. They could not go on a honeymoon, though, for fear of losing their jobs, and anyway, they could not have afforded one. They moved in with Edith's parents.

Three years later, when they were expecting their first child, on 11th March 1938, they were glued to the radio listening to the news about the German troops invading Austria. Church bells tolled to greet the invaders. Edith watched Hitler appearing on the balcony of the Imperial Hotel opposite the Bristol, where she worked. The crowd kept cheering and asking him to stay on the balcony.

When Edith went to work the next morning, she was told that she no longer had a job. Her note said: "Dismissed – reason Jewish". The hotel's staff was quickly changed, too. The Jewish director disappeared. Edith demanded compensation from the new director, but she was refused.

On 18th March, only four days after Hitler entered Vienna, the persecution of Jewish people began. Amid these terrifying events, Walter's big sister, Ruth, was born on 4th May 1938.

The whole family was trying to find a way to get away from Austria. They could have become domestic servants in England, but because of having baby Ruth, this was not possible. Kurt worked as a vocational teacher of radio engineering, which was in high demand. So, they still had food on the table, but one morning, the black-uniformed soldiers of the Gestapo knocked on their door. They took Edith and her baby to their headquarters for interrogation.

'What am I accused of?' She asked the commandant.

'Communist activities.'

Edith now realised what a big mistake it was to ask for compensation for her dismissal. 'This is not true. Please phone the hotel for witnesses,' she demanded. Baby Ruth in her arms started to wail. Edith was locked into an empty room to nurse her. Through the window, she saw her colleagues from the hotel arriving. They waved at her, but she turned away. She thought that they were against her. After an agonising hour spent waiting, the commandant called her into the office.

'You are a very lucky young woman,' he said. 'Most people in your situation would be on their way to the concentration camp in Dachau, but you may go home now!'

Edith scurried home, but she was terrified. It was clear that they were no longer safe in Austria. Trying to find a country that would take them in as immigrants, Kurt and Edith wrote dozens of letters to radio factories in Europe, but it turned out that Estonia was the only country that allowed visitors without a visa. They decided to flee. They had to buy return tickets to Tallinn, the capital of Estonia, to avoid suspicion.

The family of three left Vienna on 28 September 1938 and after stops in Berlin, Konigsberg, Danzig Kovno, and Riga they arrived in Tallinn. At each station, their passports and luggage were checked, and they panicked, trying not to show it.

In Tallinn at the airport, the radio factory's director Mr. Itskovits met them. Their worried relatives back in Vienna had sent a telegram to the chief rabbi of the Tallinn Jewish community which said: "Woman and baby arriving. Please help when landed."

Kurt became a cherished engineer in the radio factory and Edith looked after Ruth at home. As city people, Edith and Kurt now had to learn to adjust to life in the country. They had to grow vegetables, kill chickens for meat and find pleasure in the simple things of life, such as sunshine, wind, and nature. The radio still provided music and they made friends who spoke German and Yiddish. Edith learnt to speak the Estonian language. She started a button-making industry at home. She covered the buttons with textiles and delivered them to dressmakers.

The last letter they received from Vienna informed Edith and Kurt about other members of the Sekules family. Edith's sister Lotte, and Walter's grandmother Miriam were able to find work in England. Kurt's parents were lucky to emigrate to Northern Ireland where they joined a British government scheme to establish a new business. The saddest of the news was that Edith's father and grandmother both remained in Vienna and died.

Walter was born in April 1940 in Tallinn. On the eighth day of his life, following Jewish tradition, he was circumcised, in the interest of cleanliness. Cleanliness was observed in food, too. Jewish people were very selective about what they ate. Meat from pigs, rabbits, squirrels, camels, kangaroos, and horses or predator or scavenger birds such as eagles, owls, gulls and hawks were not considered "kosher" or clean. There was a celebration afterwards with a lovely, kosher meal and singing.

The family of four spent a few happy months in Tallinn with the family Itskovits, but war was around the corner, following them like a shadow.

Joseph Stalin, the leader of the Soviet Union, the most powerful country in the East, and Adolf Hitler, the leader of the Third Reich, the most powerful war machine in the West, made a secret pact that gave territories to the Russians as part of a deal for not attacking the German army. Russian planes appeared in the sky over Tallinn in June 1940 and all the Baltic States, including Estonia, became part of the Soviet Union. For Edith and Kurt, this was all too reminiscent of the occupation of Austria, but their neighbours tried to console them, 'Don't worry. The Russians are humane. It will be all right.'

Yet, everything changed. The Soviet state took over all the factories, including the radio factory where Kurt worked. The living space of each person was decreed at nine square metres, the size of three single beds. If somebody had more, someone else was moved into the building with them. The well-to-do factory owners, the Itskovits, lost their business and their house and they had to move into one room together.

On the morning of the 15th of June, Edith heard the news that all the business owners were rounded up and sent to Siberia. Edith and Kurt ran to the Itskovits, but they were gone from their apartment. The couple rushed to the railway station where they found masses of people crammed into cattle cars. They ran up and down on the platform, shouting 'Itskovits!' till they found them. They managed to say goodbye through the tiny window of the cattle car and pressed some money and a watch into Mrs Itskovits's hand before the train took off.

Edith and Kurt knew that they only had a short time before they would be deported as well, so they started to prepare. They bought luggage with leather straps and started to stock provisions.

On the 22nd of June 1941, Hitler broke the pact, and the German Army attacked the Soviet Union. As soon as this happened, Edith, Kurt, Ruth and baby Walter became Enemy Aliens. Although they were civilians, they were regarded as enemies, because their country was now part of Germany which was at war with the Soviet Union.

A few days later a Soviet officer appeared at their door. The parents did not speak Russian, but a neighbour translated for them, 'Pack what you need for a year away from here,' he said.

When the officer saw what they had packed, he called a lorry. While they were preparing to leave, they heard sirens.

'Into the cellar!' The officer shouted. They ran and huddled together on coal boxes under spider nets in the cold cellar and waited until the German airplanes flew by. Finally, when the lorry was loaded, they had to sit on their belongings on top of it. Walter was fourteen months and Ruth was three years old. After a short journey, they arrived in the first camp for Enemy Aliens, near Tallinn. The camp was a collection of nationalities and languages. Most of the prisoners were Austrian, Czech, German, Slovak, half of them Jewish refugees from Austria and Germany. Women and children were locked up separately from the men at night. When she was taken to the toilet by a guard at night, Edith realised for the first time that she was a prisoner.

The German Army advanced fast into Estonia. As the war progressed, the Enemy Aliens were moved further east by train. After two and a half-thousand-mile journey with shorter and longer stays in different camps, they arrived in Kok Uzek, Karaganda, Kazakhstan, Siberia.

Walter

From his early beginnings, the only camp Walter could remember was Kok Uzek. They arrived there in January 1943. The camp had a watchtower on each corner guarded by a soldier. There were four barracks for women and children and one large barracks for men. When they arrived there, all those buildings were covered by snow.

Through corridors, dug out between high walls of snow, they were led into a bathhouse to get washed. There was no running water or a shower, but huge wooden tubs. An old man ladled the hot water into it from a cauldron. The hot water made Walter's skin bright red. Mother scrubbed the children down, then she washed her hair with a yellow paste. The children's heads were shaved to avoid lice. Both Ruth and Walter looked like real prisoners now, but Mother called them 'my little tadpoles.'

The Family Barracks had many smaller rooms, but they were very tight. There was a raised platform in each corner – one for each mother and their children. In

11

one corner slept Mother, Ruth and Walter. In another corner, a German woman, her mother, and her young son, Victor lived. In another corner was a Polish woman and her son and in the fourth an Estonian woman, Frau Faust with a son, who was nine and a daughter, Eva who was eleven. Frau Faust was the only one who did not speak German, but Mother spoke Estonian and they understood each other. This lady was very clever with lighting the fire and took on the job immediately. She went to the next room and brought some embers in a bucket. She placed them inside the stove with a coal shovel and put some wood on it. When they burnt with high flames, she put coal on top. The fire started slowly, but soon enough the iron became warm. 'We have to keep the fire burning all night, it's too cold,' said Frau Faust and the mothers agreed to take turns.

In the middle of the room hung an electric light tube over the wood and coal-burning stove, but it was switched off soon. Walter and Ruth helped Mother push their boxes and leather bags under the sleeping platform.

'Time for bed,' Mother said. Walter jumped into the corner and fell on a sack filled with straw. The grey blankets they were given had horsehair sticking out between the felt, scratching but Mother still had her fur coat from Tallinn. She covered Walter and Ruth with it. They snuggled into their corner and fell asleep.

The next morning, they had Appell. Everybody had to stand at the end of their beds and a Russian soldier came in to count them.

After this roll call, Walter went to the door, peeping out at the snow, trying to find out more about their new camp. He saw huge animals arriving at one of the buildings. They were tall, hairy and had a hump. Their mouths had huge teeth and their breath swirled in clouds around their heads.

'What's that animal called, Mother?' Walter asked.

'Dromedary,' Mother replied.

The dromedaries brought large packages on their backs to the Kitchen Barracks. Women came out of the building and started to carry the boxes in, supervised by a soldier. He was a tall man in a white padded uniform and a red star in the middle of his flappy-eared cap. He had a rifle thrown over his shoulder. When he saw Walter, he signed to him to come closer, out of the barracks. When Walter approached him, he thumped his chest and said, 'Sasha,' and Walter understood that this was his name. He thumped his chest and said, 'Walter'.

Walter's mother was watching them and now called out. 'It's not safe to stay outside now, the frost is dangerous. Come in and help me, Walter.' Walter ran inside.

In the room, Mother Ruth and Walter unpacked their belongings, the silver cutlery, her little pots and pans, and the flour she still had from Tallinn. They brought in snow in pots. Mother melted the snow on the stove and mixed it into the flour. She kneaded the dough, then rolled it out and fried a flatbread. The smell of that made them all feel at home, even though they only had tea to wash it down with. It was wonderful.

Nourished and now full of energy, Ruth and Walter played "tadpoles". They lay down on their stomach on the platform and wriggled their legs facing each other, pretending to swim.

'Now we're grown up,' Ruth shouted. She sprang off and jumped around on the floor like a frog. Walter joined her and croaked. When Ruth got bored, she went to play with the other children from the other corners. Eva, Victor and Ruth played cards, but Walter was not interested. When she saw him standing around, Mother took out a sock full of buttons from her suitcase and gave it to Walter.

'Look, Walter, you can play with them.'

The buttons were left over from Mother's button industry in Tallinn. Now they became Walter's main toy. He sorted them by colour, size, pattern, or material on the wooden boards of their bed. He liked putting them in order. He grouped them by size or colour, in rising or falling order, and he created shapes with them.

They met Father at lunchtime in the Canteen Barracks. The meal was bread with kasha – a kind of oatmeal soup. The children got a cube of sugar and a piece of butter, too.

'Everything for the children!' Father said, smiling.

'Can you show me where you sleep, Father?' Walter asked.

'Jawohl,' Father replied.

Through another corridor cut into the snow, they walked to the Men's Barracks. It was full of bunk beds on both sides of the walls with three wooden stoves in the middle.

Father pointed at a mountain of snow in the direction of a watch tower.

'That's my workplace, the Engineers' Barracks. We can't go there now, but I'll show it when the snow is gone, I promise.'

'What are you doing there?' Walter wanted to know.

'I must guard and maintain the radio,' Father said, 'but at night, I have shepherding duties. I will have to guard the cattle and horses outside the camp so that they don't run away and get eaten by wolves.'

Walter thought it was amazing that his father could do so many things. He was a guard, too. Just like Sasha, only without a rifle.

Father took Walter back to the Family Barracks and said goodnight. Soon, it was Appell again. They heard the clinging of metal on metal. Sasha came into their room and counted them. He winked at Walter and saluted. Walter grinned at him and did the same.

Spring

The winter days passed but spring arrived slowly. The camp authorities gave people shoes made of rubber tyres, which was useful, as everything was covered in mud where you could sink in too deeply. The men laid wooden planks over bigger holes, and you had to balance over them in the yard. With the snow melted, they could see the three layers of the wire perimeter fence now. A lower, a higher and one more, even higher. The soldiers guarded the gate.

A stream ran at the bottom of the camp and next to it, there was a hill. On the top of the hill, a piece of rail was suspended from a high frame. When a soldier hit it hard with a hammer, you could hear the sound in the whole camp. In the morning it was sounded to wake you up, and in the evening, it signalled the switching of the electric light.

From early March on the sun shone bright all day. The yard dried up and thin grass started to grow here and there. Walter met Father every morning at the gate when he arrived back from his shepherding duties.

Horses were used for ploughing the fields. Every adult had to work. Some of the women had to keep the camp clean, work in the kitchen or repair clothes and the fishermen's nets and work in the laundry. The men mostly worked in the field or did whatever the Commandant and his soldiers ordered. Sometimes they had to chop wood or help the women in the laundry. The wringing was hard work. Two people had to hold up a sheet and twist it in opposite directions until all the water was squeezed out of it for drying.

The children had to go to school. Frau Adler was their teacher in the School Barracks. Ruth, Eva and Victor went to school together every morning. Walter should have gone to the nursery, but he did not like it. He thought he was too old to spend his days with little children. He preferred to go on expeditions.

Walter's favourite place in the camp was the Barracks Under Construction, a half-finished building that always had some novelty to offer. Walter often sneaked in there to explore the ground. He found many forgotten things there, such as rusty nails or even a golden bullet case that he added to his button collection.

Apart from the Hospital Barracks and the Canteen Barracks, the camp had a Bathhouse where they could wash once a week. There was a WC building, too. It was a large shed with a long trench covered by thin boards. You could sit on the board or squat over the hole emptying your bowels into the trench. Of course, it filled quickly, and it smelled. It had to be emptied on occasions by the men. The manure was used as fertiliser in the fields. On such days, Father would say, 'I'm on 4712 duty today'.

'Why do you call it 4712, Father?' Walter wanted to know.

'U-4712 is a German submarine, my son,' he said laughing, 'but luckily, I don't have to dive in too deep.'

Every family had a small vegetable patch behind the Family Barracks. They soon found out that in the neighbouring room, a Romanian woman had seeds. Mother swapped a towel for some. Ruth and Walter helped her to soften the ground with their coal shovel and sow the seeds. It was Walter's job to water the soil if it was too dry. He checked the patch every morning. Soon, some shoots appeared and started to grow, and the red tops of young carrots peeped out from the ground.

On a sunny warm day, when he was playing alone in the yard, Walter saw a carrot, and he thought it was time. He pulled it out, washed it in the stream and munched on it. He was delighted. It tasted fresh and sweet. He was skimping happily on his exploratory round in the yard when a woman he knew from the neighbouring room crossed his way.

'You thief, come here!'

Walter went to the lady.

'You have stolen my carrot!'

Walter shook his head, but when he looked down, he realised. He pulled the carrot from the neighbour's patch! The lady grabbed him by the arm and marched with him to the Laundry, where Mother worked. 'Your child is a thief!' The woman shouted.

'I'm sorry, he is too young. Perhaps, he was mistaken,' Mother said, wiping her hand on her apron.

'Whatever! Teach him manners!' The woman said, letting go of Walter's arm at last.

Mother turned to Walter and waved her finger at him. 'Remember, always ask before taking anything!'

'Yes, Mother,' Walter said and slipped away before he could be sent to the nursery as a punishment. He was upset. He wanted to run away and never return. But how? It was impossible!

He heard chattering from the direction of the school and his sorrow turned to joy. School is finished; Ruth will be out to play. He decided that just for today he would be good and play with Ruth whatever she wanted.

'What did you do today?' He asked his sister when she came out through the dark door of the school into the bright light of the yard.

'We painted. I'll show you.'

Ruth took Walter by the hand, and they entered the School Barracks. On a large blackboard, he saw animals that he did not know the name of and fruit he had never tasted in his life. He recognised carrots, frogs, ducks and a camel with two humps. Ruth started to name the things, one by one, 'Cockerel, hen, turkey, duck, hare, camel, horse, elephant!'

'Elephant?'

'Yes. And look, this is a kangaroo and apples.'

'Apples?'

'Yes, they grow on trees, Frau Adler said.'

'I have never seen a tree.'

'You have. You just can't remember. Frau Adler says so, too.'

Walter was amazed. 'Which one did you paint?'

'I painted the squirrel and the wolf. Look!'

She showed the animal that looked like a dog.

'I want to go to school, too,' Walter said.

'When you are older.' Ruth said turning on her heel, 'Let's go to the wire.'

'Yes,' Walter said, remembering his promise.

They came out again into the heat and sunshine and climbed the hill together. They sat down on the thin grass to observe their neighbours, the Japanese prisoners of war through the wire fence. They had a similar-looking camp, with long wooden barracks, but they were all men, no women, or children. They seemed mysterious in their green uniforms, green caps, and black hair. Walter and Ruth were trying to figure out why they always did the same thing. The men kept walking in their yard round and round in a circle, folding their hands behind their backs, with lowered heads, staring at their shoes.

'Why are they doing that?' Ruth asked Father when he came to fetch them for dinner.

'I think it's an exercise.'

'It seems useless,' Walter said.

'At least we don't have to do that,' Father said.

'Look, their caps have yellow stars,' Ruth said.

'Are they Enemy Aliens?' Walter asked.

'No, they are prisoners of war,' Father said.

'So, they are just the enemy?' Ruth asked.

'No longer. They are our fellowmen,' Father said.

After the storm

One morning in springtime, Ruth shook Walter awake.

'What was that?' she asked. Then he heard it too, a high-pitched wail.

'Was it a puppy?' Ruth asked.

Walter stretched and rolled onto his side. 'No, none of the watchdogs has puppies at the moment,' he replied with a yawn, 'perhaps a crow.' He pushed his ear against the wooden wall of the barracks but there was only silence now. Whatever it was, it stopped.

'Nothing,' Walter shrugged.

'Fine. I'll go and help Mother and you go and get Father,' Ruth said, ordering him around, just like a soldier.

Mother was standing under the electric light rod in the middle of the room at the stove. She was boiling water for tea in a large kettle. The rod made a zizzing sound. Walter looked up and counted twelve dead flies stuck to it. Two more than last night. Walter often wondered why they died, but now there was no time. Father would be home soon. He jumped down from the bunk, reached under the bed and pulled out his shirt and shorts from the storage box. He dressed quickly. He put on his shoes and skipped to Mother.

'Guten morgen, Mutter,' he said, which meant "good morning, Mother".

Mother stroked his short brush of hair and pointed at the triangular wooden cuckoo clock on the wall, 'Be quick, it's nearly time for breakfast.'

Walter ran out into the yard. He avoided the vegetable patch and the puddles. Screech! He heard it again from the direction of the Barracks Under Construction. In its door stood his friend, Sasha, the soldier. Walter usually understood Sasha, even though they did not speak the same language.

Sasha had his rifle on his back. His padded white uniform was tightened with a belt on his lean stomach. He drew his flapped hat with the red star in the middle tightly over his brows. When their eyes met Sasha signalled Walter to come to him.

The Barracks Under Construction had no boards on the windows. The wind blew across it, which was pleasant in the heat of summer but too cold in winter. As they entered the building, Walter's shirt billowed. A strong drought swept his hat off his head. He caught it just in time. Then he saw where the noise was coming from. In a large wooden crate, two chicks were squawking. The birds had white fluffy feathers all over, black at the ends of their wings. They opened and closed their beaks, making that high-pitched wail.

Sasha winked at Walter.

'They must be hungry,' Walter said and then he noticed his rumbling stomach. He tapped at his belly and signalled to Sasha that he had to go for breakfast. Sasha nodded.

Walter left the Barracks Under Construction and ran to the gate, which was guarded by two soldiers who had guns. These men were local, from Kazakhstan. They pulled the heavy gate open to let Father in.

'Good morning.'

'Good morning, Walter,' Father replied.

They walked on together towards the Canteen Barracks and met Ruth and Mother, in the middle of the yard.

They entered the Canteen Barracks and joined the line. When it was their turn, they took their tin mugs with tea and a slice of bread and settled around a table. Walter warmed his hands on his mug, chewing his bread slowly to make it last longer.

'I was worried about you, Kurt,' Mother said to Father. 'The wind was howling all night.'

Father nodded and Walter noticed his bloodshot eyes.

'Yes, it was a wild storm. The lightning scared a horse, and it broke its leg. They shot it at the end.'

'Oh,' Mother said.

'No,' Ruth said, starting to cry.

Walter thought it was silly to cry about a dead horse when there were hungry birds in the Barracks Under Construction. He was wondering whether to save some of his bread for them, but Mother was watching with hawks' eyes. She always made sure that they ate everything they were given.

Hunting

After breakfast, Walter took Father to see the birds. 'These are eagle fledglings,' Father said. 'Their parents must have got lost in the storm.'

'They seem very hungry,' Walter said. 'What would they eat?'

'Meat.'

'What?'

They never had any meat. Dried fish was the main dish they had during the day with the soup his mother dismissively called 'gruel'.

'You know, like *suslik*,' Father said. Walter remembered. He had *suslik* a long time ago, but he didn't know it was meat. People caught those animals sometimes in the field. They were very tiny and very fast. He didn't like it very much.

'You could try worms and mice,' Father suggested.

'Is that kosher?' Walter asked.

'Of course, not,' Father said. 'Eagles don't care about that.'

Walter was thinking. Could he find meat in the Canteen Barracks? He often loitered around there between mealtimes.

He ran there, to see. Six dromedaries had just arrived. Their backs were packed with boxes full of groceries. Sasha was there, to make sure that all was done in order.

The animals got down on their front two knees and then they dropped their bottoms on the ground, too. The women on Canteen duty came out and unloaded the boxes, and carried them in. Walter waited patiently. When all the boxes had been taken down, Sasha winked at him.

This was the sign Walter was waiting for. There was a spot between the animal's shoulders and the hump, where Walter could snuggle in. Then Sasha took the reins and made the animal stand up. Walter had to grab the dromedary's coat so as not to fall. Sasha led the dromedary around in the yard to Walter's delight. The animal rocked him. After one round he wanted more, but he knew that Sasha would not allow it. He had to get down. He saluted Sasha to thank him, and he grinned.

Walter drew circles on his tummy and made squawking noises to make Sasha understand that he was looking for food for the birds. Sasha shook his head. Not from the Canteen Barracks. He led Walter to a big stone in the shadow of the barracks. He kicked the stone with his heavy boot and turned it over. There were three long worms under the stone. So this was it!

Walter found a further ten worms under the stones in the yard. He collected them in his cap and returned to the birds. They swallowed them in no time. Then they squawked again.

'Thirteen worms are nothing,' Walter thought.

He ran to the Engineer's Barracks where Father worked during the day.

'Please, Father, help me to catch a mouse!'

Father laughed. 'Well, I can't claim to be as clever as a cat, but I can help you to make a mousetrap.'

He took a piece of board, and a spring and found some wire. Father even had a piece of bread that he had kept for later. Walter made little balls of bait from this bread for the mice.

They placed the mousetrap in the corner of the building.

'Now you must wait. With some luck, you will have a mouse by tomorrow.'

The next morning, Walter ran to check, and there was a dead rat trapped. Walter ran to Sasha, who had a very sharp knife. He cut up the dead rat and chopped the meat into small bites for the eagles. Walter was allowed to feed the birds, but when they started to pinch his fingers, he stopped. Sasha brought a tin plate and offered the meat to the birds on it instead.

Malaria

The summer was hot and wet in Siberia. The rain quickly turned the fields into swamps and the mosquitoes feasted on people. Walter became ill. One minute he was shivering the next he was very hot, fighting a fever. The Camp Doctor diagnosed: Malaria.

He gave Walter bitter pills that made everything yellow. His skin, his saliva and even the white of his eyes.

'Yellowman, fellowman,' his sister Ruth teased, but Walter was not impressed. He had to stay in the Hospital Barracks with other sick people. He missed his friend Sasha, and he was wondering what was happening to the eagles. Would Sasha feed them well? Did he have time to hunt for mice alongside his guarding duties? Sometimes he heard screeching. When he looked out through the window, he saw crows on the roof.

His only pastime was playing with his button collection in the hospital. He kept it in the head of an old sock. He lined up his buttons like people sometimes stood in lines in the camp: the Soldiers, the Enemy Aliens, the Jews, and the Japanese war prisoners next door. The different nationalities: Estonians, Romanians, Germans, Polish, Spaniards and Austrians like Mother and Father. Walter was not sure what his nationality was, but he spoke German. In the hospital, he had too much time to think, but too much thinking gave him a headache.

Ruth visited him on her way home from school every day. She brought her writing materials with her: a wooden board and a nail.

'Frau Adler allowed me to teach you,' Ruth said proudly.

The board was painted black and Ruth was able to scratch the letters of the alphabet onto it with the nail. Walter learnt a new letter every day. He copied and 'wrote' them with his buttons.

When he was allowed to return home, the days were already getting shorter. Walter ran to the Barracks Under Construction. He tore the door open and stepped inside, but nearly ran out again.

The birds were huge now. They had turned brown all over and ran around in the barracks flapping their wings and balancing on their curved talons.

When they saw Walter, they came to him, quaking and begging for food. Walter staggered backwards and bumped into Sasha who had just appeared at the door. When he saw Walter's cringing, he laughed and signalled with his hand to follow him.

Normally, Walter was not allowed to cross the stream, which was the natural border of the camp. On the other side was the field, not a place for children. Now he followed Sasha, all excited. They balanced on the plank that served as a bridge over the stream. Walter spotted leeches and fish in the water underneath.

Adults were working in the field, harvesting the cabbage. They cut them and threw them from hand to hand building a chain. It looked like fun.

Walter watched Sasha. On the edge of the patch, near the ditch, Sasha kept bending down. He lifted metal hoops, one by one. At the third such hoop, there was an animal trapped.

'A hare,' Walter cried out, remembering the paintings in the school.

Sasha freed the dead body and held it by the legs. Its floppy ears were sweeping the ground. Sasha made quaking sounds and Walter understood. The hare was food for the eagles. On their way back, when Walter was balancing on the plank, Sasha stopped at the other end and shook it, laughing. Walter was scared. He nearly fell into the water, but he grinned bravely. Sasha was a funny man.

At dinner, when Walter told the story of the hare to Father, he said,

'I'm surprised Sasha did not take the hare home to eat. Some people say it tastes nice.'

'Like suslik, Father?' Walter asked.

'I don't know, my son. We don't eat that. It's not considered kosher.'

'Is fish kosher, Father?'

'Yes, and chicken. What would I give to eat some chicken breast!'

~

Soon it was autumn. Frost covered the ground in the early mornings like a whitewash. Walter still complained about headaches.

'Take him over to the Japanese camp to get his eyes tested,' the Camp Doctor ordered.

Mother and Walter, guarded by Sasha the soldier, paid a visit to the neighbouring Japanese war prisoner camp.

The Japanese doctor had a round mirror attached to his forehead. With one free eye and the other peering through the little hole in the mirror, he examined Walter's nose and ears. Then Walter had to read letters on a board fixed on the door. He was so proud that he was able to read each letter. He did not need any glasses, but for good measure, the doctor checked his teeth. Then he said something to Mother in a different language.

'It's all good, your molars are growing,' Mother said to Walter.

The Japanese doctor took out a twig from a box and handed it to Walter. He signalled to him to chew on it. It tasted sweet.

'It's liquorice,' Mother explained.

On their way back they stopped at a heap of clothing, confiscated Japanese uniforms. A soldier pulled a cart out of a barracks nearby. Mother and Walter loaded the uniforms on it and pulled the cart to their camp. Some of the green coats had golden buttons and a red stripe with embroidered stars on the shoulder flaps.

'Could I have one, Mother, please?' He asked his mother, but she just shook her head.

They delivered the clothes to the Laundry. Sasha gave Mother five pieces of dirty woollen underwear, clearly taken from the Japanese soldiers.

'Spassiva,' she said with a big smile. Walter could not understand. The golden buttons would have been much more important.

When they got home, Mother laid the clothes out on the table. Ruth was just as appalled as Walter. 'Why did you bring all this home? They're disgusting!'

'Oh, children, wait and see until I wash them and unravel them!' Mother said.

'Look, what I got,' said Walter to Ruth, showing her his new chewing twig. She was jealous. 'Let me taste it,' she begged.

'Well, just a little,' Walter agreed. Ruth tasted it. 'Yummy,' she said. Walter took it back quickly. 'It's my medicine.'

Mother washed and hung up the garments in the yard and the wind blew them dry. The next day she unwound them with the help of Ruth and Walter pulling the pieces. Mother held the bobbin, Walter held one of the pants and ran with it to the other end of the room. Mother made many balls of wool and started to knit with her long needles brought from Vienna. The clicking of the knitting needles seemed to be in a race with the ticking of the cuckoo clock on the wall, only to be interrupted by the cuckoo jumping out and telling the time.

The garment was steadily growing day by day into a large rectangular shape. 'A cardigan for Father,' Mother announced, 'it will be ready by Yom Kippur.'

Bravery

Yom Kippur was the holiest of days for the Jewish refugees, towards the end of September, but the Commandant did not give the Jews a holiday. They had to work on the field, as it was a Tuesday.

Later, towards the end of October, when it was cold early in the evenings, the Russians became excited. Everybody had to clean and prepare for their celebration. The fronts and the backs of the houses had to be swept twice a day and even the dromedaries' coats got brushed. All of them, the prisoners and animals, soldiers and workers had to celebrate the anniversary of the Great October Revolution.

When it was all clean and ready, the Commandant walked around and confiscated every knife and sharp object the Enemy Aliens had. When he came into Walter's family barracks the Commandant stopped in front of Mother, who was knitting.

'Obysk,' the Commandant shouted pointing at the knitting needles.

Mother protested. 'They cannot do any harm,' she said.

The Commandant, who had bulging red eyes and was always swaying on his feet, said clearly 'Nyet,' which meant "no" in Russian. He took away the needles together with all the knives, forks and scissors kept on the table.

Even eating became difficult without the knives. They had to tear the bread into pieces.

Walter knew where they kept the confiscated objects. In the Barracks Under Construction, which was often used as a storage room.

'I know how to get them back,' Walter said, but the adults accepted the confiscation as a rule.

'Sharp objects, knives and weapons are searched in every factory and every camp in the whole of the Soviet Union around this time, before the celebration of the Great Revolution,' Dr Prenzlau said. He was one of Mother's friends, a tall, bald man with a bushy moustache.

'Why?' Walter wanted to know.

'They think that they could be used as weapons. They don't want any more revolutions,' said Dr Prenzlau, beaming a smile under his moustache.

Walter did not want another revolution, either, but he agreed with Mother. Knitting needles could not do any harm. He decided to go on a mission and get back the needles.

He was small and often unnoticed. He waited to see when Sasha would be on duty to guard the door. He hoped that even if he was caught, Sasha would let him get away with it. Sasha was his friend.

Walter knew that Sasha often took a cigarette break. When smoking he became distracted. He disappeared in the smoke and his thoughts, looking at the sky, or into the darkness, humming a song to himself.

It was getting dark. The moon was still round, sitting on top of the Watchtower like a fat bottom on the latrine. Walter knew that he had very little time to complete his mission. Mother would notice that he was missing. To worry Mother, was not part of his plan. He snuck up to the Barracks Under Construction and waited patiently.

When he heard Sasha singing the song, "Kakalinka", he knew it was time. He ran to the back of the Barracks Under Construction. He moved a loose board to the side and crept inside. The moonlight was shining through the slits of the unfinished roof into the room, glinting on the metal objects in a big wooden box. He found his mother's shiny knitting needles on the top of knives and razor blades. He hid them under his coat and ran home.

In their Family Barracks, the adults were sitting around the table. They were playing cards. Walter crept up to Mother's side and laid the needles onto her lap under the table.

Mother shouted, 'Dear God, Walter! What have you done?'

Everybody stopped playing and looked at Walter, who was barely taller than the table.

'I got them back for you, Mother.'

Mother smiled, but she was still a bit scared. 'Don't ever do that again,' she said, hugging Walter tightly.

'Bravo!' Dr Prenzlau clapped his hands. 'Bravo! Walter deserves a reward for his bravery. Come here, boy.'

Walter stepped closer. With a sudden move, Dr Prenzlau reached behind Walter's ear and pulled out something as if by magic.

Walter saw a glimmer in the corner of his eye and his heart started to beat faster. Dr Prenzlau held out a fist. 'Here you are.'

Walter stretched out his arm and opened his palm. Dr Prenzlau dropped a shining golden button into it. It was from the Japanese uniforms. A wonderful new item for Walter's button collection.

Walter watched Sasha and his soldier comrades celebrating. They danced squatting and jumping their traditional dance, the Cossack. It looked great. They drank vodka and ate bacon – made of pig – that he knew was not kosher. Yet, the adults in the barracks did not celebrate. They played cards and remembered "better times". Father talked about Vienna and Mother remembered the Opera House and Puccini, an Italian composer. 'Wouldn't it be wonderful if we could go home?' She asked.

~

November came and not only frost, but sometimes snow started to cover the ground in the mornings. Sasha opened the barracks' door and shooed the eagle fledglings out into the yard. Walter and Sasha ran at them and whoosh, they lifted themselves up into the sky. The birds first only flew to the roof, later they ventured further.

They did this every morning. Walter was worried that the birds might starve, but one day, one of the birds returned with a field mouse in its beak.

'Suslik,' Sasha said laughing.

The eagle let his brother have some of its prey. Sasha clapped. 'Hurushow,' he said. Walter knew this word. It meant – good. When they were sure that the birds had learnt to hunt for themselves, Walter and Sasha left the door open. Now the birds were allowed to walk in and out of the Barracks Under Construction as they pleased. They could return to the nest in the coal crate, and they were free to fly to hunt. They flew higher and higher – often circling above the camp for hours. They were free to go and free to return. 'If only, I could fly,' Walter thought.

Wolves!

It was still pitch dark when Walter was woken by a familiar whistle and a flash of bright light. He climbed up to peep through the window and saw the daylight rocket as it crossed the sky and fell to earth. On its way, it lit up the Watchtower, the wire fence and even the field behind it. 'I'll look for it in the morning,' Walter decided, then he snuggled back into bed on the side of his sister, Ruth.

After lunch in the Canteen Barracks, Mother and her friends had their school group meeting. Dr Prenzlau was their teacher. He was not a medical doctor, but a doctor of legal studies. The adults turned their voices down at these meetings. Victor, who was at least fourteen years old, but still lived in the Family Barracks, was allowed to join them. Walter could not understand a word they were saying to each other.

'Are you talking in a secret language, Mother?' Walter asked.

'No, Walter. We're learning English. You can pick it up, too, if you listen.'

While the adults studied, the children played quietly or did their homework. Walter kept looking out of the window trying to find the direction where he saw the daylight rocket falling last night. He planned that when the time was right, and nobody noticed he would sneak out and find it.

Then he heard Dr Prenzlau saying:

'Did you see the rocket last night?'

'Yes. One of those desperate Spaniards tried to escape,' an adult said.

'Where to? Is he mad? The next station is Mongolia.'

'The watchdogs tore him to pieces,' Victor said, 'his body is laid out in the Commandant's room.'

'Sshh, the children,' Mother said, looking in Walter's direction.

'Too late,' said Dr Prenzlau, turning to Walter.

'Never go close to the wire, remember?' Dr Prenzlau waved his index finger at Walter and then he started to howl like a wolf. Auuuu!

They often heard the real wolves howling. One morning, Walter was waiting for Father at the gate as usual, but he did not arrive. After standing around for a while, watching the steam of his breath in the air, Walter joined Mother and Ruth and they took their breakfast in the Canteen Barracks without Father. A whisper rolled around in the room and finally, a man called Franz explained it loudly: 'We came home in the middle of the night, for we heard the howling of wolves. Kurt stayed behind.'

Mother took a big breath in and gripped the edge of the table.

Ruth cried as a matter of habit. Walter sat and ate his breakfast. No, it was not possible that Father would be torn to pieces by wolves like that Spaniard was torn to pieces by the dogs. Father was always on the good side. Something deep in him said that his father was all right.

They took Father's bread portion and folded it into a handkerchief for later. As Ruth was still sad, Mother walked her and Walter to school passing the Family Buildings and the Men's Barracks.

'Be good,' Mother called after Ruth. Walter tagged at Mother's sleeve.

'Please, I don't want to go to play school today,' he begged.

'Then you have to help me in the laundry,' Mother replied, and Walter squeezed her hand.

On their way towards the steaming laundry, at the Engineers' Housing, they heard a commotion. The door sprang open and Father stepped out, like the cuckoo from the clock. He shouted, 'Guten Morgen!'

'Kurt,' Mother jumped and Walter could see the tears of joy in her eyes.

Father came down the steps and hugged Mother. Then he lifted Walter to hug him, too.

'What happened, Father? Did you fight the wolves?' Walter asked.

'No, my son. I was safe, for I stayed with the herd while the others panicked and ran home. Wolves are much more likely to attack single animals or men than a group altogether. Remember that.'

Days in Winter

Soon, the snow fell again. It came in flocks and storms, day and night. You could not see the wooden watchtowers, but you could hear the guards shout over to each other in their mother tongue. In the yard, the water in the basins froze and when Mother hung out the washing, the clothes became rigid within minutes. On the way to the WC building, the vapour of Walter's breath tightened his face so that he could hardly say a word.

The days were dark. When Walter looked out through the window, he saw black mountain goats walking over the roof of the Canteen Barracks, looking for food. It was hard to find anything. They could not bring water from the well anymore. They washed themselves rubbing their faces and hands with snow. Mother melted the snow on the stove and made tea with it.

At first, they spent all the evenings after school indoors. Ruth and Walter jumped from platform to platform, as if climbing mountains. They hopscotched between them and pretended to leap over the stream, which was now invisible outside, hiding under thick layers of snow. Walter often dreamt about the eagles. They flew high over the camp and the white land.

When the window also was covered with snow, Ruth and Walter were told to stay indoors. They did gymnastics. Being older, Ruth ruled. She ordered Walter, 'Stand on your head.' Walter did the headstand at the wall, Ruth holding his legs.

'Good man, Walter,' Victor said and Walter felt proud.

They learnt to do the cartwheel in between the platforms, although the space was very narrow. Mother exchanged some pieces of textile for a table and chairs and they were able to eat on it in the Family Barracks.

'We use our silver spoons from Vienna for eating,' Mother said, 'You can play with the wooden dishes and spoons they gave us.'

Ruth liked the wooden cutlery, with the red and blue flowers painted on them. She had a friend, Leia, the daughter of a Romanian woman, who lived in the neighbouring room. The girls played "kitchen", while Mother chatted with the Romanian lady in French. Walter just listened, sorting his buttons.

As they were stuck indoors all day, there was time for more stories, too. Ruth and Walter could ask questions about their parents' past.

'Ruth was born in Vienna, before we fled,' Mother said. This meant that Ruth was Austrian like Mother and Father.

'And me?' Walter asked.

'You were born in Tallinn, Estonia.'

Walter was worried. 'Does that make me Estonian?'

'No, my dear, you are what we are, and you will always be what we are,' Mother said.

'What are we?'

'Jewish people,' Mother said, 'but more importantly we are a family.'

'But why are we here?' Ruth asked.

'Because there is a war in Europe and we became Enemy Aliens,' Mother said.

'Why was I born in Tallinn?' Walter tapped his foot hard. He did not want to be so different.

'Because the German Army, led by a man called Adolf Hitler, invaded Austria and we had to escape. The good Estonian people took us in, and you were born in Tallinn. It's a beautiful city, too, Walter.'

'Why didn't we stay there then?'

'One day, when Hitler attacked the Soviet Union, we were transported here, because we are Austrian.'

'Oh, I remember,' Walter said.

'Yes? It was a treacherous journey. At the railway station, we were herded into cattle trucks with 25 people in each. The truck was very hot inside and I stripped you. Then the train stopped, and we heard the sound of airplanes approaching. The guards ran into the woods and left us locked in the waggon. We shouted for help, but no reply came, only the sound of approaching German Messerschmitt bombers. They attacked the train. There was a huge blast, and our waggon shook. People yelled. The children cried. Then somebody opened the door. We scampered out and ran into the woods. Because you were naked, the midges started to attack you.'

'Like the Messerschmitts the train,' Walter said.

'You screamed while we watched the planes flying away. When the attack was over the Soviet soldiers returned. I was crying because I could not see Father.'

'Was he injured?' Ruth asked worried.

'No, he was helping to put the injured people on a hospital truck.'

Ruth sighed, but she was tearful. Walter squeezed her hand. 'Father always helps,' he said proudly.

'But we are here, and we are safe now,' Mother added, hugging Ruth and Walter to herself.

At lunchtime, Dr Prenzlau told stories about his childhood in Germany. It turned out that he was an Enemy Alien as well and even more so because he was German, and Germany was the main enemy of the Soviet Union. He came from the city of Hamburg. It was hard to imagine the many houses in a row on the seashore and the port with sea trucks.

'Sea trucks? What are they?' Walter asked, imagining a huge lorry speeding on the waves.

'They are boats, you clever clogs,' Ruth said.

'They call them vessels, too. They can carry lots of things in their belly on the big oceans,' Dr Prenzlau said.

'How big?'

'The sea is so big that you cannot see anything else but blue waters.'

'Full of 4712-s,' Walter said, and everybody laughed.

'Yes, but sea trucks don't go under. They stay on the surface, and they sound like this, booooooom.' Dr Prenzlau gave out a very deep and long sound.

Victory = Pobeda

Once a week a Russian officer, whom they called Politruk, came to read out the news to the Enemy Aliens gathering in the Canteen Barracks. He was a thin man wearing a different uniform. Mother and Father always listened tensely to his news. Walter, while playing with his buttons, just eavesdropped, of course. As time passed, people sighed with relief and the Politruk shouted "pobeda". The adults clapped and shouted "victory".

One day, Walter woke to the sound of excited commotion. Then he noticed his chattering teeth. His sister's warmth on his side was missing. Ruth was already up. Half-asleep, Walter staggered to the door. At the other end of the yard, in the place of the Hospital Barracks, was a mountain of snow. Men and women shovelled a path in the middle, trying to find a way to the door. When this was done, they dug for the windows to let some light in.

Then the men gave wooden boards to the children who climbed up to the roof and slid down from the Hospital Building onto the path. Sasha was standing at the door of the Kitchen Barracks handing out pots and pans. Walter quickly put on his warm fufaika and ran there. He could sit on a big pan and slide down much faster, swishing down like a rocket.

The exercise made him and Ruth hungrier. Mother was pleased, even though she had to swap more towels for food.

~

Father was given the duty of working on the reservoir dam. He had to leave early every morning with a group of men and he only returned in the evenings.

'We have to cut holes into the ice to get water and fish for food,' he said. 'It's hard work, but I don't mind.'

On the fourth day after starting, he was brought back in a truck straight to the Hospital Barracks. He was blind. Mother was very scared, and Ruth cried.

'There's no cure or treatment for snow blindness,' said Camp Doctor, 'only time can help.'

So, time was the healer. While they waited for time to do its magic, Walter became Father's guide. They walked around together in the camp, Father laying his hand on Walter's shoulder. When he had to go to the WC Building from the Hospital Barracks, he had to take him by the hand and lead him to the ditch to make sure that he did not fall in. By now the contents were frozen, but still, nobody wanted to risk falling in. Father kept saying, 'you are my eyes, Walter, you are my eyes'.

They ate together at the table. Walter pushed the spoon under Father's fingers. He bent his head low and slurped, sometimes letting the gruel flow back without noticing.

'Sorry, Kurt, try again,' Mother said and Father sighed. He ate very slowly and Walter just watched him, eating slower, too.

When they finished their strange meals together, Father told stories about his childhood, his father, and their life in Vienna. As if being blind had helped him to see the past.

'My father had a feather factory in Vienna,' Father said.

'I thought the birds made feathers,' said Walter.

'Well, in those years, feathers were extremely fashionable. Your grandfather had a factory where they produced ostrich feathers for theatrical and evening costumes. I suppose, all useless now, in the middle of a war.'

'Oh, but all those feathers in our pillows and duvets! How I miss them.' Mother said. 'There's nothing more comfortable than sleeping covered with eiderdown. Not like these heavy blankets we must sleep on now.'

Walter dreamt about flying that night. He had thick white feathers under his black wings and flew over the camp in circles.

After a week, Father recovered his sight and was allowed to stay on-site, working as a herdsman again. In the winter the oxen and horses were kept in a stockade but had to be guarded against wolves.

A Christmas gift

It was December and the time of Hanukkah. The menorah, a candelabra with nine arms, stood in Frau Adler's room in the School Barracks.

All summer, Mother had collected beeswax for the candles. Now they took pieces of string they called wicks and dipped them into the melted beeswax to make small candles that they could stick into the menorah. Every night for eight days, members of the Jewish community flocked to the school pretending to visit Frau Adler. Since they had not been allowed to celebrate Yom Kippur, they knew that they had to keep Hanukkah secret. They lit a candle, one more every night, celebrating the growth of the light. The children got a nut or a cube of sugar as a treat and they sang songs. When all the candles glowed, it was the most beautiful sight.

A week later, the camp authorities celebrated Christmas. The dromedaries brought new packages. A gift arrived from the United States containing cooking oil, egg powder, fish powder and conserves. One of the cans had an eagle on it and Walter was reminded of his eagle fledglings again. Where could they be? He promised himself that he would ask Frau Adler, the teacher. And then he thought: Adler! Adler was the German word for eagle!

The Camp Cook prepared a feast. Mother and Father were happy. Due to his job as a radio engineer, Father was able to bring news about the Allies and the Soviet Union, who were defeating the Germans. Paris and Vienna, too, had been liberated.

'The tides are turning,' people said. But the most exciting news for Ruth and Walter was that their parents expected a baby.

Ruth made up a rhyme that she chanted all the time.

'Stork, stork, don't pester – Bring me a sister'

Walter was annoyed. There was no rhyme for brother, but he still hoped that the stork would bring him one. But he had doubts. It was winter and the storks had left in the Autumn and would only return in the spring.

Then, one day, when Mother was so big that Walter could not see her face from her tummy looking up at her, she disappeared overnight. The next morning, Walter, Ruth and Father struggled over high heaps of snow to visit the hospital building and meet their new family member. All the way to the Hospital Barracks, Walter kept wishing that it would be a boy, a little brother. The baby in

Mother's arms looked wrinkled like an old man and it was tiny.

'This is your sister Leah,' Mother said.

Walter started to scream. 'No, no, no!' Everybody looked at him amazed. Walter ran into the corner.

'Don't be silly,' Mother said.

'Let me hold her,' said Ruth and she was allowed to take the baby in her arms.

Walter stood in the corner and did not want to come any closer. There was no justice in the world. Ruth won, again. He just stared at them, the happy bunch, and it took him a while to understand that crying cannot change a thing. He had a sister.

Mother said to Father, 'She has your nose, Kurt.' Walter came closer and examined the creature. She had a tiny little nose, nothing like Father's. Then he laughed.

Mother and baby Leah had to stay in the hospital for two weeks. While Mother was away, Father looked after Walter and Ruth in the Family Barracks. It was fun. Father knew so many things.

'You see, Walter,' he said pulling down the cone hanging on an iron chain on the cuckoo clock, 'This is gravity. Two weights make the whole thing work and tell us the time.' Father took down the clock, turned it over and opened a little door at the back. 'You see, there are cogged wheels here that move the hands on the face of the clock. It's a Swiss invention, but I can see the Russians like it, too.'

Walter touched the metal wheels. They felt cold. The rest of the clock was made of wood, even the hands. Walter remembered the question he always wanted to ask, but there had never been time.

'Can you tell why there are dead flies on the electric rod?' Walter asked Father.

'Well, because of the 'direct current' in the electrical supply. It's dangerous to touch. You could stick to it and die. It could kill you so don't ever try.'

When the camp radio had to be repaired, Father was called and he took Walter with him. Father soldered some wires together and the crackling sound returned like magic. The voice of a man said something in Russian.

Mother and baby Leah arrived home equipped with a cot, a wooden tub and a big bag of muslin for nappies. From now on Mother was excused from work duty and stayed with her children in the Family Barracks. Little Leah took up much of her time. Feeding and nappy change and washing was the constant order of the day.

Father took the children to school in the mornings. Walter was allowed to attend school at last and all at once he felt so much better. With Frau Adler's help, the children examined the huge map on the wall. Frau Adler was able to read

Russian letters, which were very different from German. She took a long stick and pointed at the places on the large map.

'This is Austria, and here is Vienna,' Frau Adler pointed at a brown spot on the map. 'It's brown because of the Alp mountains.'

'Here is Hamburg, where Dr Prenzlau came from,' shouted Ruth.

Walter pointed at the big blue area above it. 'And that's the sea.'

A little further on along the big water, there was Tallinn and Estonia, but they could not find the town of Karaganda, where their camp was.

'I guess because it is too small,' Frau Adler said, 'but look, this is Kazakhstan.'

Neither the red lines around green areas nor the strange Russian letters said anything to Walter. Kazakhstan was a big green blot on the map.

'On old maps, there were white areas, too,' Frau Adler said, 'which signalled uncharted territories. Places where no man has ever been. Look, here. This is Siberia.'

With her long stick, she pointed at an area just above Kazakhstan. Walter looked out of the window, and he could only see white. Snow covered the ground still, although it was nearly April. Maps did not make any sense.

'Frau Adler, would you know where eagles live in winter?' He asked.

'Yes, I do. Eagles have their nests in the tall pine trees. Unlike storks, they never fly to Africa.'

The war is over!

The 20th of April 1945 was a big day in history. The Russian army bombed Berlin, the capital of Germany on Hitler's birthday which also happened to be Walter's birthday. While the Russian soldiers and the Commandant kept shouting "pobeda", or "victory", Walter and his family celebrated his birthday in the Family Barracks with singing, carrot juice and toffee. Sasha dropped in and gave Walter a toy that he had carved himself. It was a wooden sheep. The sheep fitted Walter's palm exactly. He was delighted.

As the days passed, more captured soldiers arrived and the Soviets created a new camp nearby for the German prisoners of war. Walter watched them through the barbed wire fence and often listened to their songs that wafted over on the wind.

The news they heard at mealtimes became more cheerful. In May 1945 the War was over in Europe. Everybody danced and sang, and the Russian soldiers even hugged and kissed the Enemy Aliens.

Father and Mother squeezed their children to their chests and said, 'We can go home.'

Walter was wondering what that meant. No soldiers? He immediately thought about his friend, Sasha. Will we have to leave him here? And what was that place 'home'? He knew no other home than their corner of the family room.

Summer came with its heat and work in the field. The stream dried up and water was delivered to the camp laundry in lorries. In August, many more Japanese war prisoners arrived in the neighbouring Spaski camp and they came to the barbed wire to barter. They wanted food for their belongings. Mother took carrots from the vegetable patch and exchanged them for long silk vests, underpants, and gym shoes. To her delight, Mother got more underwear to unravel.

When Walter and Ruth saw the black shoes, they started to scream. The big toes were separated from the rest! Like the hoofs of goats!

'This could only belong to demons,' Ruth shouted when Father put a pair on.

'Please don't,' Walter tried to stop him, but Father only laughed. He walked around in the shoes and tried to pinch Mother's wool between his toes.

'These are gym shoes, Walter. Imagine how easy it would be to climb up a rope or a pole or even a tree with them.'

There were no trees in the camp, so this was difficult to imagine, but when a pair of wooden clogs with straps turned up as well, the shoes with a gap between the toes started to make more sense.

As the war was now over in Europe, the Enemy Aliens could mingle with the German prisoners of war, too. None of the prisoners had their markings on their jackets, some of them had black, others green uniforms. They noticed how much better fed they were. The Germans did not have to work so they staged a musical production, to which all the Enemy Aliens were invited. On a platform that served as a stage, the men sang in a choir. Ruth and Walter sat squashed between their parents and had a wonderful time. They understood every word.

Fighting with the pen

The war was over, everybody knew. Yet, the Enemy Aliens were still waiting for their travelling documents to arrive. After another long winter, in May 1946, they got a big scare. The Austrian Enemy Aliens, together with the German prisoners of war, were ordered to go and work in a coal mine near Karaganda. This was unheard of and against agreements between nations. The adults shouted about slavery and many men hid in the Family Barracks or outdoors in the grass if they could find a place to hide.

Father started a hunger strike. He did not eat for days.

'You're very strong, Mr Sekules,' Victor said. Although he was already sixteen years old, he was still growing and always hungry.

After seeing that Father refused to be separated from his family, the Commandant relented. Father was allowed to stay at home. Dr Prenzlau was not so lucky. He was a single man. The soldiers came with dogs and took the men away, including Victor, who was too tall not to be noticed.

The women went to the School Barracks and asked Frau Adler to help. She spoke Russian and as a teacher was respected by the Russian Commandant. She wrote a long letter to the Chief Commandant. She explained that the Enemy Aliens were not fascists or Nazis. They were grateful to Russia for saving their lives, but they were the victims of war, not the perpetrators.

A week later a delegate of Generals arrived in the camp from Moscow. Walter had never seen such fat men before. Frau Adler showed them the school and explained that the children were taught to grow up as anti-fascists.

'What does that mean?' Walter asked Ruth.

'It means that we are not like Mr Hitler,' Ruth replied.

Frau Adler gave a speech in Russian which lasted for three hours. The General argued: 'Whoever has a German passport is German.'

But Frau Adler pointed out another German war prisoner and said, 'If Mr Mahler would be in your place now, I most probably would not be alive.'

'And where is your husband, Madame?' Asked the General.

'I am not talking for my husband, but for all the German Jews taken to the mines,' she said.

'Well, bravo, Madame Adler,' said the General and the delegation left.

Three weeks later the Politurk brought the news that Frau Adler's petition was successful.

'You see, children, the pen is mightier than the sword,' Frau Adler said at dinner. 'We won.'

She won her fight with the pen. All the Jewish men who had been taken to work in the mine were allowed to come back to the camp.

They arrived slowly, in groups of threes and fours. Most of them were ill. Dr Prenzlau was in a bad condition. Mother and Walter visited him in the Hospital Barracks.

'I've heard weeks ago that Frau Adler's petition was accepted,' Dr Prenzlau said between coughs.

'So, the jungle post worked,' Mother said. 'We sent you word to give you hope.'

'Thank you. I am ever so grateful.'

'What's wrong with you, Dr Prenzlau?' Walter asked.

'I have pneumonia,' Dr Prenzlau said.

'Can't you howl anymore?' Walter asked, remembering that Dr Prenzlau's favourite performance was howling like a wolf. Dr Prenzlau winked at him and waved to come closer. Walter pushed his ear to his mouth and Dr Prenzlau whispered, 'ho-ho-ho-howl.' Walter grinned, but Dr Prenzlau's wheezing was worrisome. They said goodbye with a handshake. 'I will be fine,' Dr Prenzlau promised.

On their way home to the Family Barracks, Walter asked Mother, 'What is that: Jungle Post?'

'That's a way of messaging. I tell you lots of messages and when you meet someone next you tell them all and then they go and tell them to someone else, and finally, the message will get to the person you meant it for. As we have no paper to write letters, this is how we send messages to each other.'

'But we have the newspaper.'

'Newspaper is full of printed letters, and it is used for rolling cigarettes, lighting the fire or wiping your bum, but we never get any empty sheets of paper.'

'I see,' Walter said, being reminded of the sheets he saw in Frau Adler's room at school. Frau Adler kept the few pages in the drawer and used the blackboard with chalk instead and the children wrote with nails on black painted wooden boards. They had no paper to waste. The few books they got in the Library were handed around and were read and read again.

'I see,' Walter agreed. 'Books should never be wasted for messages when you can use the jungle mail.'

When Dr Prenzlau finally left the hospital, Mother prepared a special meal for his birthday. She asked people working in the field to bring some meat. All they could find was a ram's testicles! They asked Frau Adler whether that was kosher.

'I found nothing against testicles in the Talmud,' she said, 'but even so, in the interest of Dr Prenzlau's recovery, perhaps we could make an exception'. Mother's dish was delicious and it made everybody laugh.

A birthday party

Summer arrived at last. By the time the cabbage was blooming in the field, Dr Prenzlau recovered. Even though he had lost a lot of weight, he was able to work on the field again.

On 8th June, Mother's 30th birthday was to be celebrated in the hut. Mother invited all her friends and asked them to bring a party piece.

Walter and Ruth went out into the yard and hid in the shadow of the Barracks Under Construction. The party piece had to be a surprise.

'I want to be an eagle,' Walter said to Ruth.

'Nah, you do that all the time. You run around with open arms like an eagle. There is nothing special about that. We must perform something new.'

'Well, what about a dance?' Walter asked.

Ruth became excited. 'Yes! I'll sing "Kakalinka" and you'll dance the Cossack,' she said.

Folding his arms in front of his chest Walter squatted down and jumped from one foot to the other. It was hard. He came out of breath very quickly.

'Go on,' Ruth said, 'it's just like gymnastics.'

'You try it,' Walter said, but he knew very well that it was a boy's dance. He decided to master it, no matter what. He practised for hours on end. When Sasha spotted him jumping around in the yard, he laughed. He squatted on Walter's side and showed him how to do it properly. Doing it together was much more fun.

On the morning of Mother's birthday party, Ruth and Walter helped Mother to make the cake. Mother called it "miracle cake".

Recipe for a miracle cake:
Ingredients:
White bread soaked in goat milk
Sugar cubes are crushed and mixed into the dough
Beetroot grated

Cook the mixture on top of the stove for twenty minutes – always stirring.

Grease the inside of a bowl with lard if you have some. Mix the dough and squeeze it into it. Let it cool and settle for an hour. When set and cold, turn over the bowl and let the cake slip onto a plate. Decorate it with cherries or thin carrot rings.

Voilá = finished = Fertig!

People started to arrive and sat down around the big table. The meal was the ordinary rations plus some cherries, strawberries and carrots. It was a feast!

The party pieces were amazing. Dr Prenzlau recited poems. Father sang an old Viennese tune. Frau Adler read a poem she wrote for Mother. Walter and Ruth were rewarded with loud applause for their dance performance.

~

The summer passed quickly. Preparing for the journey 'home', Mother did nothing but knitting. She made more jumpers. Each member of the family got a cap, scarf and mittens.

One night they were invited to the neighbouring camp for a cinema show. Chairs were lined up in front of a whitewashed wall and a machine with a lens at its end was brought in. The machinist put two big reels one over the other on its side and fixed the film in between them. Walter was amazed. He could not follow the action on the screen. He stared at the machine instead. When Father noticed, he whispered, 'It's a projection, Walter, I'll explain it later. Now watch the film.'

That night Father played a shadow play on the wall in the barracks in the light of a candle. He could form animals with his hands and the children had to guess what they were. He held his fist up against the light and a rugged shadow appeared on the wall.

'A wolf,' Ruth cried.

To tell the truth, Walter had never seen a wolf, only heard them howling. He had a carved wooden sheep from Sasha. It was fat and woolly.

'A sheep,' Walter said.

'Yes, it is,' Father agreed and then he added, 'Well, Walter, this is the principle of projection.'

'Tartars'

The short autumn passed and the Enemy Aliens faced another harsh winter in Kok-Uzek. The adults were becoming impatient. They had to wait for the paperwork needed to return to Europe, which arrived at last in January 1947. The Austrian and Hungarian Enemy Aliens could finally start their journey "home". Walter was worried. What did this word mean, after all? His home was the Family Barracks in the camp, and he knew that somewhere near his eagles nested, too. Now his parents were excited about the journey.

'Our new home will be much better,' Ruth kept telling him. Walter did not understand, but the idea of a journey excited him, too.

In tears, they said goodbye to Frau Adler and Dr Prenzlau who had German passports and had to stay on longer. 'We will meet again, keep in touch,' they said. Joy mixed with sadness.

It was still the middle of winter when they left Karaganda, wearing Mother's knitted layers upon layers.

'Who cares about the cold if we're free at last?' Father said.

First, the families were loaded onto a convoy of lorries. On their way, it was stopped due to snowdrifts and the men had to get off and shovel the snow from the road.

The lorries took them to another camp where they had to spend a night waiting for the trains. Walter went on an exploratory trip and found the entrance to a cave with big rocks of coal stocked in containers outside. When he returned, everybody was alarmed.

'I thought we had lost you,' Mother said, but Walter announced proudly, 'I have been in a coal mine.'

Father and Mother just laughed, but Victor agreed. 'Yes, this is where we were working. Walter must have found the entrance.'

At the train station, they were assigned specially prepared cattle cars. Each corner had double platforms, one for each family. For the first time, Mother, Father, Walter, Ruth and Leah slept together in the same room. The car had no windows, only air vents high up. To let light in, they had to open the sliding door, but then the cold came in, too. There was a coal burner in the middle of the waggon and the fire had to be kept alive day and night.

The train moved at a fast-walking pace and often stopped to take on water and coal and to distribute food. The three thousand miles journey "home" began.

Sometimes trains passed in the opposite direction. They were so full of people, that some of them had to sit on the tops of the engines. Walter, with his little Russian, asked them, 'kuda ty ides – where are you going,' and they cheerily replied, 'domoy – home'. Walter was confused. We are going home, too, but that way. Above them, in the sky, Walter often saw eagles flying. 'Go back home, I don't want you to get lost,' Walter thought.

Sasha seemed very happy, too. Walter often saw him riding his horse alongside the train. He sang "Kakalinka" to himself. Walter and Ruth joined him singing the chorus, shouting over the clickety-cluck of the train.

When they stopped, Father went to the local markets to get food. He sometimes took too long and had to run to catch up with the train. On one occasion he did not arrive in time. They started to roll on and take up speed. Mother was worried and shouted over to the Commandant, who was on horseback. They spoke in Russian, but Walter could see how cross the Commandant was. Mother said, 'Pozhaluysta,' which Walter knew meant "please".

Swaying on his horse, the Commandant ordered Sasha and another soldier to go back for Father. He duly arrived carrying a small bag of food, on horseback riding behind Sasha. People reached out and helped Father to jump over onto the moving train.

At their next stop, still in Kazakhstan, Walter was allowed to go with Father to the market. Father had a bar of soap to sell, and he haggled with a man, in Russian. The man had eggs and bread, and Walter could already taste in his mind the scrambled eggs on toast his mother would make for dinner.

The market crowd suddenly moved apart to allow two smartly dressed youths to swagger through. They wore black cylindric hats and long gold-embroidered gowns that waved around the legs of their shiny leather boots.

'Tartars,' Father whispered.

'Teffillin'

When they returned to the waggon, Walter observed a Jewish man with a little black hat that was tied to his forehead. He was comparing this to the costume of the Tartars, but this old Jewish man was murmuring, sunk deep into his thoughts, rocking himself.

Later, when he was doing his exploratory round, Walter asked the man, 'What is that thing you put onto your head and arm every morning?'

'It's called the Teffilin. We use it for prayer.'

'What does it mean?'

'It contains scrolls of the Torah, our Bible.' He took a small black book from under his shirt and read to Walter, 'You shall put these words of mine on your heart and your soul; and you shall tie them for a sign upon your arm, and they shall be as totafot between your eyes.'

Walter was confused. He had never heard this word, either. 'Can I try it?' Walter asked.

'When you are older, you might.'

Walter spent most of the day sitting at the sliding door, looking at the landscape. It was an endless long flat and empty land. He liked watching trains full of battered tanks, lorries and other broken materials of war.

One day there was great excitement amongst the travellers.

'We are approaching the Volga River,' Mother said.

The river was enormous. Walter had never seen so much water before. A long bridge crossed over it and big plates of ice floated on the surface below them.

'We are back in Europe,' people shouted.

When they had crossed the bridge Walter was looking for a sign of Europe, but there was none. The landscape did not look any different, yet people were so happy.

In the city of Saratov, they dismounted the train and were taken to a bathhouse.

The three children were put into a bath. Walter enjoyed the hot water and soap working through his skin after such a long time crammed together. Soaking and sprinkling each other, Walter croaked like a frog and made baby Leah laugh.

Many days later they reached Stalingrad. Walter remembered the name but could see nothing else than broken houses.

His friend, Sasha the soldier, came to say goodbye.

'Dasvidanya,' Ruth and Walter chanted their goodbyes and Sasha beamed at them with his smile. He raised his hand to salute Walter and he returned the gesture.

'Goodbye.'

Europe

After passing the River Volga, the journey seemed to slow down even more in Europe. Their train was often parked in railway sidings to allow other, more important ones to pass in the opposite direction.

The next time they crossed a river it was the Dnieper in Ukraine. In every ruined village, town or city, people did nothing but work in the streets to remove the debris of war. These names of countries and the imaginary lines that divided them did not say anything to Walter. Passing yet another such line, in Romania, they had a longer stay.

Mother put her fingers into a roll of wool and pulled out a white piece of paper. When she unrolled it, Walter saw that it was scribbled full of curly letters.

'We kept this pound note all these years, but now it has a purpose,' Mother said. Father and Mother sat down to write a telegram for Father's relatives in Northern Ireland to let them know that they were alive and they were on their way back 'home'. Father waved to a man, standing on the platform. He took his hat off and came closer.

'Please, take this telegram to the next post office and send it for us. The change is yours.'

The man looked at the two pieces of paper, then he nodded and smiled.

'Jawohl,' he said.

When the man with the Tefillin saw this, he asked Father: 'How can you trust a stranger with so much money?'

Father replied, 'We have no other choice, but to trust.'

At this border station, they changed trains. From now on they were sitting on wooden chairs inside and their belongings were shoved under and over the seats. The landscape changed. They crossed many tunnels in high mountains and after a while arrived at the Hungarian border.

A Hungarian soldier came to the waggon and said in German, 'You'll get two days' respite in a prisoner-of-war camp near the border.'

The Jews from Karaganda were excited, but when they saw that the camp was full of German war prisoners, there was an uproar.

'This is an insult,' Victor said.

Mother complained to Father, 'after six and a half years in Siberian camps we have fallen into the hands of the Germans.'

Father comforted Mother, 'Look at this as a crossroads. They are going to the place where we are coming from. Try to observe this from high above, it is just a matter of time.'

That night Walter dreamt that he was still travelling on a train. The clatter of the train was still in his head. Then he became an eagle, circling over the camp that looked like the face of a wooden clock, with the hand slowly moving, ticking the rhythm of time passing.

After the respite that upset the adults so much, they travelled on another train till they reached the city of Budapest. Here they had to wait for two days on the rails. Yet, it was exciting. A huge consignment of food from the American-Jewish aid agencies awaited them. Walter ate chocolate for the first time in his life. They got so many tins of sardines that Mother and Father shared them with the Soviet soldiers.

The next station was Győr, on the Hungarian-Austrian border. Here they had to wait for their papers for many days. Ruth and Walter were invited to visit a Hungarian family, who had a bathroom with a bathtub and toilet with flushing water. Squeezing each other's hands, they stood there amazed for a few moments and Walter asked to be allowed to pull the cord again.

The lady of the house agreed, 'Jawohl,' she said.

Entering Austria the adults became tearful. When Mother glimpsed the snow-covered peaks of the Alps she burst out crying.

'Now I know we are at home at last,' she said, hugging her children.

Vienna

It was nearly springtime when they arrived in Vienna, the birthplace of their parents and Ruth. First, the family had to go to a hospital for disinfection. They sank into hot baths. The smell of it stung their noses. Their skulls were searched for lice. Then people combed white powder into their hair. Walter giggled. Ruth looked like a snowman. Suddenly, he missed the times when they were playing in the snow in Kok Uzek. A sweet sadness came over him that he did not understand. Their parents were so happy! From the hospital, they were taken by ambulance to a large school to sleep. Each classroom had four families occupying bunk beds.

'This will be our home for now,' Father said.

As the days passed, they had to say goodbye to their friends. Victor left, in search of his remaining family.

In the streets, Walter saw his first trams, buses and cars. The rumble of the city was deafening. You had to shout at each other when walking in the streets. Vienna was complicated. The city was divided into three areas, Russian, American and British. Crossing from one area to the other, they had to show their ID cards to soldiers. The identity cards they received had four languages: German, English, French and Russian. Yet Mother and Father were pleased. Now they had their identities back.

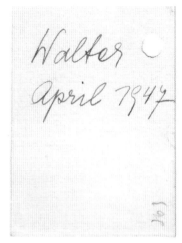

One day an old friend of Mother arrived at the school and offered them a fully furnished apartment to use free of charge. The family moved to the Hitzing district and their new home had huge rooms and even a bathroom. There was no running water in the tap, but Father filled the bath with water from a bucket so that they could have baths.

Ruth and Walter were enrolled in a local school, and their hard life began. They spoke German but could not read or write.

When they first entered the enormous classroom, Walter noticed a cane on the teacher's desk. 'What is that for?' He wondered, but then he remembered Frau Adler's long stick at the school back in the Kok Uzek camp. 'It's for pointing at the map,' he thought, although he could not see one on the wall.

Ruth was struggling with the thick pencil they had to use. She tried to draw letters but in vain. She whispered to Walter, 'It was much easier with the nail.'

'Don't talk during class!' The teacher shouted. Walter heard a hissing sound and Ruth screamed. She held her red hand to her face and started to cry.

When Walter looked up, he saw that the teacher was holding the cane in his hand.

Ruth kept crying and Walter did not dare to move. He reached to take Ruth's hand under the desk and squeezed it. He was thinking about the camp, where Frau Adler never beat them. If Sasha was here now, he thought. He would take the rifle from his shoulder and order the teacher to leave the room. 'Outside the wolves would tear him to pieces.'

At home, Ruth told Mother and Father what had happened at school that day.

Mother was upset.

'The teacher smacks other children, too,' Ruth complained, 'He has a special cane for it.'

'This had never happened in Kazakhstan,' Mother said, hugging her tightly, 'I'm sorry. Be good, Ruth, and all will be well.'

To make up for the injury that upset the whole family, Mother took the children to the Rathaus in Vienna. They had a ride on the Giant Wheel, overlooking the city. Walter saw a man wearing Lederhosen, shorts made of wild boar leather! 'I want those, too,' he thought.

Parcels arrived from New York. Walter learnt to read 'Nestlé' and enjoyed the condensed milk, corned beef and Grape Nuts. This was a cereal that had three birds on the label. The packaging had the same eagle he had seen before. American eagles! They did not look anything like his eagle fledglings back in

Siberia, but reminded him of them, nevertheless.

The whole family visited a cinema. A dark room only for projections! They watched Plisch und Plum, a film in which a teacher caned the children. Ruth started to cry.

'This was a bad idea,' Mother said to Father.

Walter could not engage with the action on the screen, but the film was in Technicolor and the colourful projection was new to him.

~

Walter spent his seventh birthday, 20th April 1947, in the hospital with Malaria. This was very different from the Hospital Barracks in Karaganda, yet much less lonely. Ruth had Malaria, too. They watched trams and cars from the window instead of eagles and tried to read a book called Struwwelpeter about a boy who had long nails and hair that he didn't like to wash. This book of rhymes was available to all children in the hospital's ward. Walter, with Ruth's help, managed to read it very quickly and asked Father to bring him more books.

He was very pleased with The Adventures of Pinocchio. First, he read the pictures, and later he managed to spell some words. The reading was slow and arduous, but it helped him to spend time and be less bored. His reading companion, Ruth, managed to get home sooner than him, which was just unfair. Ruth always won.

Walter was even more upset when he heard that Father took Ruth to the Opera House to see Aida, while he was left alone with Malaria. Walter quickly decided that Malaria, like the fox and the cat in Pinocchio, was the worst of friends.

As the fox and the cat did with Pinocchio, older boys on the ward took Walter under their wing. They were raucous and told stories about American soldiers. How they patrolled the streets and gave chocolate to children and nylon tights to women. By now, Walter knew the power of chocolate, too. How could anybody not like chocolate? The American soldiers were nice.

When Walter got out of the hospital a month later, the siblings' first photo was taken in a real photo salon. They dressed up nicely and looked like any other happy Viennese children.

It also turned out that their Father was a genius inventor.

'I have been thinking about an improvement to radios all those years in Kok-Uzek, but there was no paper to write it down.'

Now Mother typed up his improvement on a typewriter and they sent the patent on to the big radio factories, Philips, and Eindhoven.

Miracles

While Father stayed at home to look after the children, Mother visited her old place of work, the Bristol Hotel, from where she had observed Hitler standing on the balcony of the Imperial, waving to the crowd. Now, in peacetime, Mother brought news of a miracle.

'Like your miracle cake?' Walter asked.

'No, much better. A real miracle!' Mother said.

'Let's hear it,' Father said.

'The director of the Bristol Hotel is the same Jewish man again. He had been hiding with the help of friends during the war and now he got his job back!'

'That's fantastic!' Father said.

'And, he invited us for tea!'

The next day, Father was busy tutoring a young boy, so Mother took Walter and Ruth and little Leah in a perambulator, to visit the hotel and to have afternoon tea with the Director. Although they could see bullet marks on the walls the building still looked majestic.

'What did you do here, Mutter?' Ruth asked.

'First, I was a canteen help, later I had to do anything and everything, including ushering in the guests. World-famous musicians stayed here, and I collected autographs.'

'Autographs?' Walter asked.

'Pictures with signatures.'

'Where are they?'

'Gone. I had to sell them before we fled.'

~

The Director was very pleased to see Mother. While the children munched on cookies, the adults sat down to catch up with each other's news.

'We ended up in a Siberian camp as Enemy Aliens, but the Russians saved our lives,' Mother said.

'And what about your sister? I remember her well,' asked the Director.

'Lotte was accepted for nursing training in England and got away early in the summer after the occupation. She got my mother out, too. They are living in London.'

The Director nodded. 'That was the time I resigned and went into hiding. I owe my life to the courage of my friends.'

'Yes, we were all terrified because we did not know what happened to you. The Gestapo took me with my baby and accused me of communist activities because I demanded compensation for my dismissal. Luckily, my colleagues stood up for me.'

Walter and Ruth looked up from their cookies. 'Really?'

Mother nodded, 'Yes. After an hour spent waiting, the commander called me into the office and released us. My colleagues' witness statements were in my favour. My life was spared, but I could forget my request for compensation, of course.'

'Well, Edith, I think it's time that you get your compensation for this unfair dismissal,' said the Director. He went to his desk and took out a large booklet. He wrote onto a page, tore it off and handed it to Mother.

Mother looked at the piece of paper and her eyes became wet. 'Thank you, Herr Director. This is much more I could have expected. You're very generous.'

The lost sheep are found

Father's suggestion to improve radios was accepted as a patent by the radio factories. This seemed like another miracle. Now, through Mother's compensation payment and Father's invention, they had a bit of money.

People from the camp often came to visit. Father mentored a teenage boy, Walter Leitsch, whom they knew from Estonia, to help him get into university. It was important to vouch for his character and to prove to the authorities that he had not been a Nazi.

'Will I have to prove that I'm not a Nazi?' Walter asked Father.

'No, hopefully, by the time you go to university, all of this won't matter,' Father said.

One day, Father got news from Northern Ireland. Father's family had received the letter they had sent from the Romanian-Hungarian border a year before.

'So, the pound note was not wasted after all!' Mother said triumphantly.

'Can we go?' Ruth asked.

'Would you like to meet your family?'

'Yes!' Walter and Ruth shouted in unison.

'The herd will be reunited,' Father said smiling. Walter remembered Father when he returned from his sheep-guarding duty one morning, having escaped the wolves. So, this is what it meant. The family is safer when they are together.

The letter said that Father's family were delighted and there was a job waiting for both parents in Londonderry in their factory.

Now the parents were busy applying for an entry permit to the United Kingdom. After six months in Austria, the papers arrived.

Mother was packing again. Big crates were filled with wool and knitted garments. Even the old family's silver cutlery got packed away. The ones she had carried from Vienna to Tallinn, from Tallinn to Kazakhstan and from Karaganda back to Vienna. She packed it all up again, while they ate with cheap alpaca cutlery, waiting for their papers, ready to go. Their friends were coming and going, saying goodbye. One night Mother's old school friend, Katrina arrived with a small box in her bag. The minute Mother saw the thin long box, she knew what it contained.

'My goodness!' She said.

It was her inherited jewellery. 'From my grandmother!' She shouted and her eyes filled with tears.

'We kept it hidden all these years but could not get to it for half of the house was in ruins. Now that the rubble has been moved, I found it in the cellar,'

Katrina said.

'It's a lovely farewell present,' Mother hugged and kissed her friend.

Finally, at long last, in September 1947, Walter and his family were ready to go. They travelled on an overnighter train to France through the Alps. The mountains seemed mysterious and majestic. In a couple of days, they reached the sea and boarded a ship.

Walter had never seen so much water before, that waved and rocked you like a dromedary. He remembered Dr Prenzlau imitating the horn and kept booing all the way long. After many hours they saw white rocks blinking at them in the distance.

'Those are the Cliffs of Dover,' Father said. 'It's England.'

London – Derry and…

When they arrived at London Waterloo Station, Walter was greeted by his aunt Lotte and Grandmother, two ladies he had never met before, only heard of. They hugged him and did not want to let go. People cried tears of joy, even Father.

In their home, Grandmother gave each member of the family a torch and a hot water bottle. 'These are your life-savers in London,' she said.

The same night, keeping the hot water bottle on his tummy or sliding it down to his feet, Walter enjoyed the shadow plays he could create on the walls of their bedroom. Ruth held the torch and he put his thumbs together. His hands became the flapping wings.

'A bird,' Ruth said.

'Eagle,' Walter replied.

Breakfast at Grandmother's was porridge, not comparable to the gruel called "Kasha" in Karaganda. It had salt in it and sugar on top with a splash of milk.

Grandmother was still tearful at breakfast. She said, 'We were looking for you for eighteen months, and when we heard nothing, we thought you had died. I had memorial trees planted for you in Israel.'

'What kind of trees?' Walter asked.

'Olive, of course, for peace.' She pulled out a piece of paper and showed it. It was a sad-looking blue tree with low-hanging branches. Walter could spell out the name Sekules on the document and letters that were curlier and looked different, like the ones on the Menorah.

'What does that say?' He asked.

'This is in Hebrew. It says your names in loving memory.'

Walter imagined sitting under an olive tree called Walter, somewhere far away in a hot country. It was beautiful.

~

Grandma and Auntie Lotte tried to spoil the children. They went to the British Museum, and even the Greenwich Maritime Museum. Here he discovered another imaginary line that confused him. This was even weirder than the borders on land. This line is meant to propose time!

'This is Prime Meridian, longitude zero,' the guide said. 'This side is minus; this side is plus. Every 15-degree longitude represents one hour's difference in time: You can work out the time at every location on Earth if you know how many degrees it is east or west of Greenwich.'

Walter kept walking over it, wondering.

When they visited the London Zoo, he saw eagles in a tall cage. This is cruel, he thought. Eagles should be free and fly high in the sky. He thought back to his eagles. Would they have chicks by now? They visited the camels and dromedary and he saw a real elephant.

Time spent in London was fun, but it ended soon. Towards the end of October, Mother and Father received work permits to work in Uncle Robert's factory in Londonderry that produced artificial flowers. They took another train to Liverpool and crossed the Irish Sea by boat. After another long train journey, they arrived in Londonderry. Walter met his other Grandmother, Elsa, and his Uncle Robert. By November he was attending P1 in Derry Model School. As he didn't speak English, he had a hard time here, too, as well as at his first school in Vienna.

By springtime, his old friend, "Malaria", visited him again and Walter travelled back to London, to the Children's Hospital. He spent his eighth birthday looking out through the window, watching the red trams in London. Grandmother and Auntie Lotte visited him, but still, it was hard to be away from Father, Mother, Ruth and Leah. The good thing was that during the long months in the hospital, his English improved. His favourite word was "more", asking for more soup.

When he recovered, he visited the London Olympic Games in August.

August 8th

London 1948

My dear mother
I went to the olympic games in the Wembley Stadium when we arrived there were only a few people. First I saw 200 nice girls doing exercises on the lawn, afterwards came 200 young men. They doing gymnastic too. I saw the start off the Marathon runner, many kisses Ruth Lea mother father granny
your son Walter.

```
Edith Sekules          Garden City,
                       Londonderry.
                       24.th August 1948.

MY DEAR WALTERL,

I WAS VERY GLAD TO GET YOUR LETTER TO DAY
AND TO READ, THAT YOU ARE ALL RIGHT, BUT YOU
ARE A LAZY CHAP TO WRITE ONLY THE SIGNATURE
YOURSELF!
TO DAY I SAW MR. MAC CLUNE AND HE ASKED ME
ABOUT YOU. I TOLD HIM, THAT YOU ARE VERY
WELL AND WILL BE BACK AT SCHOOL MIDDLE OF
SEPTEMBER. MAY BE MRS. POLLAK, WHO IS WITH
IRENE IN VIENNA AT THE MOMENT, WILL TAKE
YOU FROM LONDON TO DERRY.
RUTH AND LEA ARE ALL RIGHT. DADY AND GRANY
AS WELL.
WHEN YOU COME BACK YOU WILL FIND A NICE NEW
PULLOVER, I KNITTED FOR YOU.

WE EAT LOTS OF VEGETABLE FROM THE GARDEN.
I THINK THE BRAMBLES WILL BE RIPE, JUST WHEN
YOU COME BACK. SO WE'LL GO AND PLUCK THEM
ALL TOGETHER.

TRY AND WRITE YOURSELF HOW YOU FEEL AND WHAT
YOU DO.

MANY KISSES FROM GRANY, DADY, RUTH AND LEA.
```

Love and kisses

Many thanks to the lady who wrote the letter for Walter.

Yours Mummy

That summer Walter went to Switzerland for a holiday. Everybody said that the clean and cold air of the Alp Mountains would help his full recovery. The Jewish Agency organised the holiday and Walter was together with other children 'like him'. This wasn't true. They were very unlike him. They all spoke very good English and seemed to know each other well, for they had been living together on a farm. This would have been a little bit like the camp in Karaganda, but Walter found out that most of the children had no parents. They came with the Kinder Transport to Northern Ireland. Their parents had sent their children away from Germany to England to save them from the Holocaust. Many of

58

the children were still hoping to be reunited with their parents or were still looking for living relatives back in Germany with the help of the Red Cross, a humanitarian organisation. Erwin, a rotund, jolly man, looked after them. He came from Vienna, like Walter's parents. He spoke German as well as English. He was very kind to Walter.

'Well, Vienna is a beautiful city,' he said.

'I have been on the Big Wheel,' Walter boasted.

'Fantastic,' Erwin replied. 'So, you know Vienna well?'

'Just a little, I lived in Siberia in a camp before we went to Vienna. I was an Enemy Alien,' said Walter, becoming shy.

'We lived on a Farm in County Down and we were Enemy Aliens here, as well,' Erwin said, 'but it is all over now. We are free.'

Walter was wondering what that meant, to be free. He thought that only the eagles in the sky could be free, but his parents kept saying the same. They were allowed to work whatever they wanted and move around. But Walter's freedom vanished. He had to go to a school where nobody understood him. Some days he missed the field, the stream and his friend, Sasha, but he was told that the camp would have been demolished by now and the only creatures that remained there were the eagles.

'You'll see, Walter, when we arrive in Switzerland, everybody will be speaking German,' Erwin said, and it was true.

The mountains in Switzerland were full of black and white cows. White fluffy clouds were drifting low in the sky like sugar puffs. Walter had a marvellous time and made some friends. The boys tried to teach him some more English words. They ate the most delicious Swiss chocolate and heard people sing in a loud cry like birds, which they called yodelling.

In September, he returned to the school in Derry, but at least he could speak a little more English.

…Home

Back in Northern Ireland, having German as your mother tongue proved to be a disadvantage. The word "Nazi" echoed in the air for a very long time.

Walter and his family moved to Kilkeel on the coast of the Irish Sea, where his mother opened a knitting factory. In his new primary school, Walter met a boy who had darker skin than most of the boys, as he came from Pakistan. The others called him "Gypsy". After overhearing Walter and Ruth talking in German, this boy started to call Walter a Nazi. Walter went home and complained about it to

Father, who said, 'Well, then you call him Gandhi.......'

When Walter returned to school and called the boy by the name of Gandhi, nothing happened. The boy kept teasing him. Walter knew too well that he was not a Nazi. This was the worst injustice he had suffered in his life so far. His annoyance grew day by day. The boy greeted him every morning with: 'Hello, Nazi", till one day, on the way home Walter lost his temper. He punched the boy and gave him a bleeding nose.

Ruth saw it and she was appalled. 'I'll tell Father,' she promised. Walter just shrugged. When they arrived in their new house, Ruth marched up to Father and said, 'Walter was fighting at school.'

Father asked Walter, 'did you?'

'Yes, I did. I'm not a Nazi and that's that.'

'You can't fight violence with violence. You go to that boy tomorrow and apologise,' Father said.

When Mother heard the news, she was just as appalled as Ruth.

'Have you ever seen your father fight?'

'No.'

'We don't. We're peaceful people.'

Walter was sulking. Nobody understood him. How can you be peaceful if others are at war with you?

He went to school the next day, expecting more punishment from the teacher or even a punch at his nose, from the boy. Yet, to his amazement, the boy called "Gypsy" came to him in class and shook his hand.

'I shouldn't have called you a Nazi,' he said.

'I shouldn't have punched you,' Walter said smiling.

Later, in the break, they forgot all about Nazis or Gandhi, playing games together. Their friendship lasted a long time and after a while, they both began to call Kilkeel "home".

The Sekules Family
Kirkeel April 1954
North Ireland

Lea 9 years, Ruth Elizabeth nearly 16 years
Walter Hillel 14 years
Baby Esther Madeleine 2 month
born february 7th 54 2 weeks old

Edith Mathilde + Kurt Arther
mother   father

Glossary

Gulag:	a system of Soviet labour camps and accompanying detention and transit camps and prisons
Kasha:	oatmeal soup
Obysk:	confiscate
Spassiva:	thank you
Pobeda:	victory
Hurushow:	good, well
Fufaika:	a padded coat
Cossack:	a Russian dance only for men
Suslik:	a meat dish on sticks
Kuda ty ides:	where are you going?
Domoy:	home
Pozhaluysta:	please
Kakalinka:	a Russian song. The refrain of the song refers to the kalinka, which is the snowball tree. It has a speedy tempo and light-hearted lyrics.
Malaria:	a serious and sometimes fatal disease caused by a parasite that commonly infects a certain type of mosquito which feeds on humans. People who get malaria are typically very sick with high fevers, shaking chills, and flu-like illness.
Synagogue:	church
Kosher:	clean
Hannuka or Channuka:	a Jewish festival of light
Menorah:	a Jewish candle holder with 9 arms
Yom Kippur:	a major religious festival for Jews such as Christmas for the Christians.
Holocaust:	a very large amount of destruction, especially by fire or heat, or the killing of very large numbers of people. The

term Holocaust has become the most common word used to describe the Nazi extermination of Jews in English and many other languages.

Appell:	roll call
Guten morgen:	good morning
Jawohl:	yes, of course
Fertig:	finished
Yiddish:	a language once spoken by Jews in an area spreading from Alsace to the Urals, influencing local languages and cultures. It neared extinction in the 20th century when it lost most of its speakers, mostly, but not only, through the Holocaust.

Acknowledgements

The author and Light Theatre Company CIC wish to thank all members of the Sekules Family, especially Richard and Melanie for their ongoing support. Special thanks to Caroline Page, who took the photo of Walter on the back cover, and to Agnes Tamcsu for the colour illustrations. The creation of this book would not be possible without the support of The National Lottery Heritage Fund, thanks to National Lottery players and the Arts Council of Northern Ireland.